cocktails

101 Fabulous Cocktails

Creating cocktails can be as simple and straight forward or as creative and artistic as you like. In order to create fabulous cocktails, you need to get to grips with the basic skills - from shaking, to pouring over a spoon. Once you've mastered these, making delicious cocktails is easy.

A cocktail normally contains one or more types of liquor and flavorings and one or more liqueurs mixed with fizzy drinks, fruit juices, sauces, honey, milk, cream or spices, etc. The cocktail became popular with Prohibition in the United States at which time the art of mixing drinks became important to mask the taste of bootlegged alcohol. After the repeal of Prohibition, the skills developed in illegal bars became widespread and so began the golden era of the cocktail, the 1930s. From the 1970s on, the popularity of vodka increased dramatically, and by the 1980s it was the predominant base for mixed drinks. Many cocktails traditionally made with gin, such as the gimlet, or the martini, may now be served by default with vodka.

If you are having a party where you plan to serve lots of different cocktails, ensure that you have plenty of the basic ingredients to hand - in some instances it will be possible to make the cocktails prior to the party and then chill them until ready to serve and don't forget that if you don't have a particular ingredient, you can probably find a suitable alternative, creating your own cocktail and maybe even giving it a name!

3

It is also a great idea to have a themed party based around say a particular base ingredient - this will also reduce the amount of potentially expensive ingredients you need to buy.

Cocktails are great for special occasions, but please always drink sensibly and remember the recommended medical weekly allowance of alcohol units is a maximum of 14 for women and 21 for men. In a lot of instances it is possible to reduce or even remove the alcohol from these recipes so that you and your friends can continue enjoying themselves.

So, down to basics, here are the explanations for certain terms and items you will see throughout the book to enable you to make creamy, fruity, spicy, icy exotic drinks to enjoy!

Blending

The most effective way of blending drinks is with an electric blender which will create a smooth ready to serve mixture. Some recipes will call for ice to be placed in the blender, in which case you should use a suitable amount of crushed ice.

Brandy snifter

The shape of this glass concentrates the alcoholic odours to the top of the glass as your hands warm the brandy. Typical Size: 17.5 oz.

Building

When building a cocktail, the ingredients are poured into the glass in which the cocktail will be served rather than pre-mixed in a mixing glass.

Champagne flute

This tulip shaped glass is designed to show off the waltzing bubbles of the wine as they brush against the side of the glass. Typical Size: 6 oz.

Citrus twists

To make a citrus twist, cut a thin slice of the citrus fruit crosswise and simply twist to serve on the side of a glass or in it.

Citrus peel spirals

To make a spiral of citrus peel, use a parer or vegetable peeler to cut away the skin, working in a circular motion. Take care not to cut into the bitter pith of the fruit.

Cocktail glass

This glass has a triangle-bowl design with a long stem, and is used for a wide range of cocktails. Typical Size: 4-12 oz.

Cocktail sticks

These are handy for spearing through pieces of fruit and cherries and needed in decoration. Wooden stick are not re-usable, but plastic cocktail sticks are, provided they are washed and boiled.

Collins glass

Shaped similarly to a highball glass, only taller, the collins glass was originally used for the line of collins gin drinks, and is now commonly used for soft drinks, alcoholic juice, and tropical and exotic juices. Typical Size: 14 oz.

Cordial glass

Small stemmed glasses used for serving small servings of your favourite liquors at times such as after a meal. Typical Size: 2 oz.

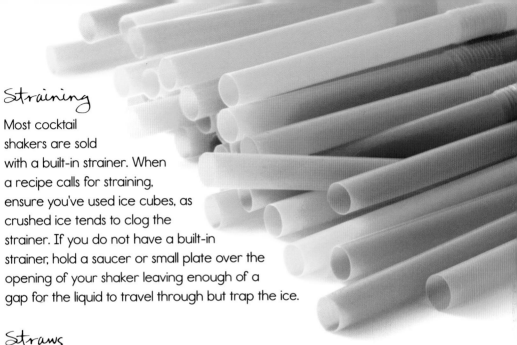

Straining

Most cocktail
shakers are sold
with a built-in strainer. When
a recipe calls for straining,
ensure you've used ice cubes, as
crushed ice tends to clog the
strainer. If you do not have a built-in
strainer, hold a saucer or small plate over the
opening of your shaker leaving enough of a
gap for the liquid to travel through but trap the ice.

Straws

Straws are of course another essential for creative cocktails.

Whiskey Sour glass

Also known as a delmonico glass, this is a stemmed, wide opening glass, similar to a small version of a champagne flute. Typical Size: 5 oz.

White wine glass

A clear, thin, stemmed glass with an elongated oval bowl tapering inward at the rim. Typical Size: 12.5 oz.

There is of course no right or wrong fully stocked bar, and a lot of what you have in your bar will be dependent upon your own personal tastes. Most or all of the ingredients below are considered a good basic bar-stock.

Liquors

Gin
Vodka
Rum (light/dark)
Whiskey
Tequila
Brandy/Cognac
Beer

Wine

White (dry)
Red (dry)
Champagne
Vermouth (dry/sweet)

Fruit

Lemon
Lime

Liqueurs

Amaretto (almond)
Blue Curacao (orange)
Chambord (raspberry)
Cointreau (orange)
Creme de Bananes (banana)
Creme de Cacao (chocolate)
Creme de Menthe (mint)
Frangelico (hazelnut)
Galliano (herb)
Goldschlager (cinnamon)
Grand Marnier (orange)
Jagermeister (herb)
Kahlua (coffee)
Midori (melon)
Sambuca (anise)
Schnapps (various flavors)
Southern Comfort (peach)
Tia Maria (coffee)
Triple Sec (orange)

Fruit Juice

Apple
Cranberry
Grapefruit
Orange
Pineapple
Tomato

Garnishes/Other

Cinnamon
Ice
Maraschino Cherries
Nutmeg
Olives (black/green)
Salt/Pepper
Sugar
Tabasco Sauce
Worcestershire Sauce

Mixers

Angosturas Bitters
Lemonade
Cola
Cream
Eggs
Ginger Ale
Grenadine
Ice Cream
Milk
Orange Bitters
Sour Mix
Tea/Coffee
Soda water
Tonic water

champagne

Alice in Wonderland

4 oz Champagne
1 splash Campari® bitters
1 sugar cube
1 drop Angostura® bitters

Put a drop of angostura bitters on a sugar cube and place in a champagne flute then slowly add the Champagne and splash of Campari.

Serve in: Champagne flute

Baby Love

1 oz Champagne
1/2 oz vodka
1/2 oz gin
1/2 oz rum
1 splash lemonade
1 splash grenadine syrup
juice of a lemon

Combine all of the ingredients together in a cocktail shaker half filled with ice and shake well. Strain over ice into a tall glass.

Serve in: Collins glass

Bellini

4 - 6 oz Champagne
1 medium ripe, peeled and pureed peach
peach slice (optional) for garnish

Stone and peel the peach, setting aside a slice for decoration and then puree in a blender. Pour the peach puree into a glass and slowly add the champagne. Stir gently and garnish with the peach slice.

Serve in: Champagne flute

Black Velvet

5 oz chilled Champagne
5 oz chilled Guiness®

Pour the Guiness equally into two champagne flutes and then carefully add the chilled Champagne, ensuring it does not mix with stout.

Serve in: Champagne flute

Blitz

4 oz Champagne
3/4 oz creme de menthe

Pour both ingredients into a champagne flute, stir, and serve.

Serve in: Champagne flute

Blue Tahoe

Champagne
4 - 5 ice cubes
1 oz tequila
1 cherry
1 oz lime juice
mint leaves
1 slice lemon
1 slice orange

Put all the ingredients together in a tall glass and then top up with chilled champagne.

Serve in: Highball glass

Bolli Stoli

3 oz Bollinger® Champagne
1 oz Stolichnaya® vodka

Pour the Bollinger into a champagne flute then slowly add the Stoli vodka, and serve.

Serve in: Champagne flute

champagne

Champagne Cocktail
Champagne, chilled
2 dashes bitters
1 sugar cube

Place one cube of sugar with the bitters in a chilled champagne flute. Fill with chilled Champagne. Add a twist of lemon peel and serve.

Serve in: Champagne flute

Champagne Fizz
3 oz Champagne, chilled
1 1/2 oz gin
1 oz lemon juice
1 tsp sugar

Pour the gin, lemon juice and sugar in a cocktail shaker half-filled with ice cubes, and shake well. Strain into a champagne flute and add Champagne.

Serve in: Champagne flute

Champagne Punch

1 bottle Champagne, chilled
4 oz Cointreau® orange liqueur
4 oz cup brandy
1/2 bottle chilled carbonated water

Combine all of the ingredients and serve chilled in punch cups.

Serve in: Punch glasses

Classic Champagne Cocktail

3 oz Champagne
1/3 oz cognac
2 dashes Angostura® bitters
1 sugar cube
lemon and orange to garnish

Place the sugar cube in a champagne flute with the Angostura bitters.
Add the chilled Champagne and cognac then squeeze in a twist of lemon
and discard. Garnish with half a slice of orange.

Serve in: Champagne flute

Fizzy Fuzzy Navel

Champagne
1 1/2 oz peach schnapps

Fizzy Fuzzy Navel/cont.
2 oz orange juice
2 ice cubes

Place the ice cubes in the glass then pour over the peach schnapps and orange juice. Fill the glass with champagne and stir gently.

Serve in: Collins glass

Grand Mimosa
Champagne
1/2 oz Grand Marnier® orange liqueur
1 splash orange juice

Pour the grand marnier into a champagne flute and fill almost to the top with Champagne then top off with fresh orange juice.

Serve in: Champagne Flute

Happy Hangover
4 oz Champagne
1/4 oz brandy
3/4 oz ruby port
3/4 oz orange juice

Shake the brandy, port and orange juice well over ice cubes in a cocktail shaker then strain into a champagne flute, fill with Champagne, and serve.

champagne

Kir Royale
5 oz Champagne
1 oz creme de cassis

Pour creme de cassis into a glass and gently pour Champagne on top. Scale the ingredients to the amount of servings for larger groups.

Serve in: Champagne flute

Mimosa
Champagne
2 oz orange juice

Pour orange juice into a collins glass over two ice cubes. Fill with chilled champagne, stir very gently, and serve.

Serve in: Collins glass

23

Pink Drink

3 oz Champagne
3/4 oz strawberry liqueur
2 oz strawberry puree
1/2 oz lemon juice
1 tsp caster sugar

Rim a wine glass with strawberry liqueur and caster sugar. Blend all the ingredients (except champagne) briefly with three-quarters of a glassful of crushed ice. Pour into the glass and add Champagne. Garnish with half a strawberry and serve with short straws.

Serve in: Wine glass

Raspberry Shine

3 oz Champagne
1 oz Chambord® raspberry liqueur
1 oz Bacardi® Limon rum

Pour the Chambord and Barcadi Limon into a glass and top with chilled Champagne.

Serve in: Champagne flute

Rose of the Ritz
3 oz Champagne
1 oz cognac
1 oz raspberry liqueur
1 tsp lemon juice
15 raspberries

Blend all the ingredients (except the Champagne) well in a blender and pour into a wine glass. Add the Champagne, and serve.

Serve in: Wine glass

Strawberry Kir Royale
Champagne, chilled
20 strawberries, halved
1 tbsp sugar
1 tsp creme de cassis

Mix the strawberries and sugar in a bowl and let stand for 5-10 minutes. Stir occasionally. Divide into two glasses, add Champagne and creme de cassis.

Serve in: Wine glass

Strawberry Champagne

3 oz Champagne
3/4 oz vodka
3/4 oz strawberry brandy

Pour into a wine glass half filled with broken ice. Garnish with two halves of a strawberry, and serve.

Serve in: Wine glass

Tropical Champagne Kiss

4 oz Champagne
3/4 oz dark rum
3/4 oz orange juice
2 - 3 dashes passion-fruit syrup
2 - 3 dashes lemon juice

Combine all the ingredients (except Champagne) in a shaker with ice cubes to chill. Shake well then strain into a champagne flute, carefully fill with Champagne, and serve.

Serve in: Champagne flute

champagne

American Star

1/2 oz sloe gin
1/2 oz Amaretto® almond liqueur
1/2 oz Southern Comfort® peach liqueur
1 splash orange juice
1 splash sweet and sour mix

Pour all of the ingredients into a cocktail shaker with a handful of ice cubes and shake until completely cold. Strain into a glass and serve. Sweet and sour mix is a blend of lemon juice and syrup. It is often just referred to as sour mix, and should be readily available, but it is very easy to make your own. Mix eight ounces of lemon juice with two tablespoons of sugar.

Serve in: Old-Fashioned glass

Angel's Delight

3/4 oz gin
3/4 oz triple sec
1 1/2 oz cream
2 - 3 dashes grenadine syrup

Put all the ingredients in a cocktail shaker half filled with ice cubes. Shake well and then strain into a cocktail glass, and serve.

Serve in: Cocktail glass

Aperitivo

2 1/4 oz gin
3/4 oz white sambuca
3 dashes orange bitters

Pour gin, sambuca and bitters into a mixing glass half filled with ice cubes. Stir well. Strain into a chilled cocktail glass, garnish with a twist of orange peel, and serve.

Serve in: Cocktail glass

Blue Moon Martini

1 1/2 oz Bombay Sapphire® gin
3/4 oz Blue Curacao liqueur

Put the gin and the Blue Curacao in a cocktail shaker with lots of ice. Shake with ice and strain into a cocktail glass. Garnish with a twist of lemon.

Serve in: Cocktail glass

Dirty Martini

2 oz gin
1 tbsp dry vermouth
2 tbsp olive juice
2 olives

Place an ice cube and a small amount of water in a cocktail glass and then chill in the freezer for about 2 - 3 minutes. Combine all of the ingredients including the olives

Dirty Martini/Cont.

in a cocktail shaker, cover and shake hard 3 - 4 times. Remove the cocktail glass from the freezer and empty the ice then strain the cocktail from the mixer into the glass. Garnish with the olives.

Serve in: Cocktail glass

Dry Martini

1 2/3 oz gin
1/3 oz dry vermouth
1 olive

Stir the gin and vermouth with ice in a mixing glass. Strain into a cocktail glass, add the olive, and serve.

Serve in: Cocktail glass

Gimlet

2 oz gin
1/2 oz Rose's® lime juice
1 lime wedge

Pour the gin and lime juice into a shaker half filled with ice cubes, then stir rather than shake. Strain into a cocktail glass and garnish with the lime wedge.

Serve in: Cocktail glass

Gin Fizz

2 oz gin
juice of 1/2 lemon
1 tsp powdered sugar
carbonated water

Placed the gin, lemon juice, and powdered sugar with ice into a cocktail shaker and shake well. Strain into a highball glass over two ice cubes. Fill with carbonated water, stir, and serve.

Serve in: Highball glass

Long Island Iced Tea

1 oz gin
1 oz vodka
1 oz tequila
1 oz rum
1 oz triple sec
1 splash Coca-Cola®

Mix the ingredients together over ice in a glass. Pour into a shaker and give one brisk shake. Pour back into the glass and make sure there is a touch of fizz at the top. Garnish with lemon.

Serve in: Collins glass

Negroni Cocktail

1 oz gin
1 oz sweet vermouth
1 oz Campari® bitters
slice of orange (optional) for garnish
soda water (optional)

Stir with ice and strain into a chilled cocktail glass
3/4 filled with ice. Add a splash of soda water if
desired. Garnish with a half slice of orange.

Serve in: Cocktail glass

Perfect 10

2 oz Tanqueray 10® gin
1 oz Midori®
1 oz pineapple juice
1 oz ginger ale
1 oz Chambord®

Pour all of the ingredients into a cocktail shaker
with lots of ice and shake well. Strain into a glass
and serve very chilled.

Serve in: Cocktail glass

Pimm's Cup

1 shot Pimm's® gin
lemonade
1 slice cucumber
1 twist lemon peel

Pour the pimm's no.1 into a highball glass, then add a twist of lemon and fill with lemonade. Garnish with a slice of cucumber and orange if desired,

Serve in: Highball glass

Pineapple Plaza

3/4 oz gin
3/4 oz dry vermouth
3/4 oz sweet vermouth
1 pineapple slice

Shake all ingredients (except pineapple slice) with ice in a shaker and then strain into a cocktail glass. Add the slice of pineapple and serve.

Serve in: Cocktail glass

gin

Pink Lady

1 1/2 oz gin
1 tsp grenadine syrup
1 tsp single cream

Mix all of the ingredients together in a cocktail shaker with ice cubes and shake well. Strain into a cocktail glass, and serve.

Serve in: Cocktail glass

Pixie Stick

1 1/2 oz gin
1 1/2 oz Midori® melon liqueur
lemonade

Pour the gin and Midori over ice in a collins glass. Add a straw, and serve.

Serve in: Collins glass

Raspberry Release

2 oz gin
3 oz ginger ale
1 oz Chambord® raspberry liqueur

Pour all of the ingredients into a brandy snifter. Stir, and serve.

Serve in: Brandy snifter

Red Lion

2 oz Tanqueray® gin
2 oz Grand Marnier® orange liqueur
1 oz orange juice
1 oz lemon juice
caster sugar

Mix all of the ingredients (except the caster sugar) together in a cocktail shaker with ice cubes and shake well. Moisten the rim of a glass with water or juice, dip in caster sugar, and strain the cocktail into the glass.

Serve in: Highball glass

Silver King

1 1/2 oz gin
juice of 1/4 lemons
1/2 tsp powdered sugar
2 dashes orange bitters
1 egg white

Shake all of the ingredients with ice, strain into a cocktail glass, and serve.

Serve in: Cocktail glass

Singapore Sling

1 oz gin
1/2 oz Grenadine® syrup
1 oz gin
soda water
1/2 oz cherry brandy
1 maraschino cherry

Pour the Grenadine into the bottom of a collins glass, and fill with ice. Add the gin, and almost fill with chilled soda water. Top with cherry brandy, and serve unstirred, garnished with a cherry.

Serve in: Collins glass

Sloe Comfortable Screw

3 oz sloe gin
3 oz Southern Comfort® peach liqueur
3 oz orange juice
3 oz vodka

Put all the ingredients in a cocktail shaker and shake well. Serve in a highball glass with ice.

Serve in: Highball glass

Sloe Comfortable Screw, Again

1 oz sloe gin
1/2 oz Southern Comfort® peach liqueur
orange juice
1/2 oz Galliano® herbal liqueur

Add the southern comfort to the sloe gin, and fill with orange juice. Float galliano on top, decorate with a cherry, and serve.

Serve in: Highball glass

Sloe Gin Fizz

1 oz sloe gin
1 oz gin
3/4 oz fresh lemon juice
1 oz simple syrup
3 - 4 oz soda water
cherry and orange to garnish

To make the simple syrup you will need 2 parts sugar and 1 part water. Bring the water to a boil and dissolve the sugar in the water. Once the sugar is dissolved completely, remove the pan from the heat. Allow to cool completely and bottle. Shake the gin, lemon juice and simple syrup with ice and strain into an ice filled highball glass. Top with soda, garnish with a slice of orange and a cherry, and serve.

Serve in: Highball glass

Sloeberry Cocktail

2 oz sloe gin
1 dash bitters

Stir ingredients with ice, strain into a cocktail glass, and serve.

Serve in: Cocktail glass

Slow Screw

1 oz sloe gin
orange juice

Pour sloe gin into a highball glass filled with ice. Fill with orange juice, stir well, and serve.

Serve in: Highball glass

Smile Cocktail

1 oz gin
1 oz grenadine syrup
1/2 tsp lemon juice

Put all the ingredients in a cocktail shaker with ice and shake well. Strain into a cocktail glass, and serve.

Serve in: Cocktail glass

Spicy Martini
5 oz gin
1 oz vermouth
15 drops Tabasco® sauce

Shake the gin and vermouth with ice in a cocktail shaker. Pour into a
cocktail glass and add the Tabasco into the finished drink. Stir very lightly.

Serve in: Cocktail glass

Snake In The Grass
2 oz gin
2 oz Cointreau® orange liqueur
2 oz vermouth
2 oz lemon juice
1 maraschino cherry

Pour all of the ingredients (except the cherry) into a cocktail shaker with lots of ice and
shake well. Strain into a glass, garnish with a cherry, and serve very chilled.

Serve in: Cocktail glass

Strawberry Martini

1 1/2 - 2 oz gin
1 tsp dry vermouth
1 tsp Rose's® grenadine syrup
sugar
2 strawberries

Rub the rim of a chilled cocktail glass with a cut strawberry then dip the rim into a bowl of sugar until evenly coated. Pour the gin, vermouth, and grenadine into a mixing glass with plenty of ice, and stir briskly. Strain into a cocktail glass and drop in a strawberry.

Serve in: Cocktail glass

Super Supreme

1 1/2 oz gin
3/4 oz peach brandy
3/4 oz orange juice
1 tsp egg white
1 dash Angostura® bitters

Put all of the ingredients together with ice into a cocktail shaker and shake well. Strain into a cocktail glass filled with crushed ice, and serve.

Serve in: Cocktail glass

Raspberry Martini

1 1/2 - 2 oz gin
1 tsp dry vermouth
1 tsp Rose's® grenadine syrup
sugar
4 raspberries

Rub the rim of a chilled cocktail glass with a cut raspberry then dip the rim into a bowl of sugar until evenly coated. Pour the gin, vermouth, and grenadine into a mixing glass with plenty of ice, and stir briskly. Strain into a cocktail glass and drop in the remaining raspberries. Garnish with a cherry and slice of orange.

Serve in: Cocktail glass

Tailspin Charlie

3/4 oz gin
3/4 oz sweet vermouth
3/4 oz Green Chartreuse®
1 dash orange bitters
1 twist lemon peel
1 maraschino cherry

Stir all ingredients (except cherry) with ice in a mixing glass and then strain into a cocktail glass. Top with the cherry and serve.

Serve in: Cocktail glass

Tanqueray and Tonic

2 oz Tanqueray® gin
1 oz tonic water
1 slice lime

Put a couple of ice cubes in a glass and fill 2/3 of the way up with Tanqueray Gin. Fill the remaining 1/3 with tonic water. Add lime.

Serve in: Old-Fashioned glass

gin

Tom Collins
2 oz gin
1 oz lemon juice
1 tsp caster sugar
3 oz club soda
1 maraschino cherry
1 slice orange

In a shaker half filled with ice cubes,
combine the gin, lemon juice, and sugar.
Shake well. Strain into a collins glass almost
filled with ice cubes. Add the club soda.
Stir and garnish with the cherry and the
orange slice.

Serve in: Collins glass

Try As I Might
3/4 oz gin
3/4 oz dry vermouth
3/4 oz sweet vermouth

Put all the ingredients into a mixing glass
with ice and stir. Strain into a cocktail glass.

Serve in: Cocktail glass

Tuxedo Junction

1 1/2 oz gin
1 1/2 oz dry vermouth
1/4 tsp maraschino liqueur
1/4 tsp anis liqueur
2 dashes orange bitters
1 maraschino cherry

Stir all of the ingredients (except the cherry) with ice in a mixing glass, then strain into a cocktail glass. Top with the cherry and serve.

Serve in: Cocktail glass

Venom

2 1/2 oz gin
1 tbsp cocoa powder
2 tbsp sugar

Pour the gin over ice cubes into a cocktail shaker then stir in the cocoa and sugar, mix together and shake. Pour into a champagne flute glass, and serve.

Serve in: Champagne flute

Waikiki Woo

3/4 oz gin
3/4 oz triple sec
1 tbsp pineapple juice

Shake all ingredients with ice in a cocktail shaker then strain into a cocktail glass.

Serve in: Cocktail glass

Wedding Bells

3/4 oz gin
1 oz Dubonnet® Rouge vermouth
2 tsp cherry brandy
1 tbsp orange juice
1 dash orange bitters

Pour the gin, Dubonnet, cherry brandy, orange juice and orange bitters into a cocktail shaker half filled with ice cubes. Shake well, strain into a cocktail glass, and serve.

Serve in: Cocktail glass

White Gin Smoothie

2 1/2 oz gin
1 dash white wine
1/2 oz maraschino cherries

White Gin Smoothie/Cont.
Blend all of the ingredients together in a blender until smooth. Add a little extra white wine if necessary. Serve in a chilled wine goblet.

Serve in: Wine glass

Wimbledon Cup
1 oz Pimm's® gin
1 oz gin
1/2 oz strawberry syrup
1 oz mandarin juice
1 oz double cream

Place all the ingredients together in a cocktail shaker with ice then shake well. Strain and serve in a cocktail glass.

Serve in: Cocktail glass

Wonder Why?
1 1/2 oz gin
3/4 oz Cointreau®
1 oz pineapple juice

Shake together with ice in a cocktail shaker. Strain into a chilled cocktail glass.

Serve in: Cocktail glass

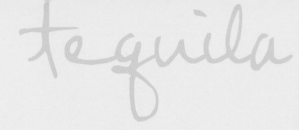

Acapulco Vision

1 oz gold tequila
1/2 oz coconut cream
2 oz orange juice
1 tbsp cinnamon

Combine all ingredients in a cocktail shaker half filled with ice cubes. Shake well, and pour into a cocktail glass. Dust with cinnamon, and serve.

Serve in: Cocktail glass

Aztec Gold

3 oz gold tequila
1 1/2 oz creme de bananes
1 1/2 oz Amaretto® almond liqueur
1 1/2 oz Galliano®
lime (optional) for garnish

Combine all the ingredients in a cocktail shaker half filled with ice and shake well. Strain into a cocktail glass and serve with a lime twist.

Serve in: Cocktail glass

Banana Margarita

1 oz creme de bananes

1 oz gold tequila

1/2 oz triple sec

3/4 oz lemon juice

1/4 mashed banana

caster sugar

Apply lemon juice to the rim of a cocktail glass, and dip into caster sugar. Blend the ingredients together with a cup of crushed ice and then place in the dipped cocktail glass.

Serve in: Cocktail glass

Black Monday

2 oz Mozart® Black chocolate liqueur

2 oz white tequila

2 oz triple sec

1 dash fresh lime juice

dry sparkling wine

Shake ingredients (except dry sparkling wine) and pour into a champagne flute. Top with dry sparkling wine, and serve.

Serve in: Champagne flute

Charlie's Angel

1 1/2 oz mezcal
1 oz Grand Marnier® orange liqueur
1 dash orange bitters
1 oz orange juice
1 oz grapefruit juice
soda water
lime

Pour all the ingredients (except soda water) into a cocktail shaker half filled with ice and mix well. Pour into a glass half filled with ice. Squeeze and drop one fresh lime wedge into the glass and fill up with soda water.

Serve in: Highball glass

Cranberry Margarita

1 1/2 oz Jose Cuervo® Especial gold tequila
1 splash cranberry juice
3/4 oz triple sec
juice of 1/2 limes
3/4 oz Grand Marnier®

Shake all of the ingredients (except the Grand Marnier) in a pint glass. Rim a margarita glass with salt and transfer the mixture. Float the Gran Marnier.

Serve in: Margarita glass or cocktail glass

Frozen Margarita

2 tsp coarse salt
1 lime wedge
3 oz white tequila
1 oz triple sec
2 oz lime juice
1 cup crushed ice

Place salt in a saucer. Rub the rim of a cocktail glass with lime wedge and dip the glass into salt to coat rim thoroughly. Pour the tequila, triple sec, lime juice, and crushed ice into a blender. Blend well at high speed. Pour into a cocktail glass.

Serve in: Margarita glass or cocktail glass

Frozen Strawberry Margarita

1 oz silver tequila
1/2 oz triple sec
1/2 oz Rose's® lime juice
1/4 oz lemon juice
1/2 oz strawberry liqueur
strawberry for garnish

Pour all of the ingredients into a blender and blend with crushed ice then transfer to a margarita glass and garnish with a fresh strawberry.

Serve in: Margarita glass

Fuzzy Pierced Navel

1 oz tequila
1 1/2 oz peach schnapps
6 oz orange juice

Half fill a tall glass with ice cubes and then pour over the tequila, schnapps and orange juice. Stir and serve.

Serve in: Collins glass

Gold Margarita

1 1/2 oz gold tequila
1/2 oz Cointreau® orange liqueur
juice of 1/2 a lime
2 tsp coarse salt

Place salt in a saucer. Rub the rim of a cocktail glass with lime wedge and dip the glass into salt to coat rim thoroughly. Combine the ingredients in a cocktail shaker, shake with ice and strain into a salt rimmed cocktail glass. Garnish with a lime wedge.

Serve in: Margarita glass or cocktail glass

High Velocity

6 oz tequila

3 oz peach liqueur

1 oz Rose's® lime juice

Combine all of the ingredients together in a cocktail strainer half filled with ice and shake well. Strain into a chilled glass, and serve.

Serve in: Margarita glass or cocktail glass

Highland Margarita

1 1/2 oz tequila

1/2 oz Grand Marnier® orange liqueur

1/2 oz Drambuie® Scotch whisky

juice of 1/2 a lime

2 tsp coarse salt

Pour the ingredients into a cocktail shaker half-filled with ice cubes. Shake well. Pour into a salt-rimmed margarita glass, garnish with a slice of lime, and serve.

Serve in: Margarita glass or cocktail glass.

Italiano Margarita

1 oz Amaretto® almond liqueur
2 oz sweet and sour mix (see pp15)
1/2 oz Jose Cuervo® Especial gold tequila
1/2 oz triple sec

Simply pour into a mixing glass and stir. Transfer to chilled glass and add ice cubes.

Serve in: Margarita glass or cocktail glass

Love Child

4 oz tequila
12 oz Rose's® lime juice
1 tsp honey
2 dashes Angostura® bitters

Combine all ingredients in a shaker with ice. Shake then strain over one or two ice cubes in a cocktail glass, and serve.

Serve in: Margarita glass or cocktail glass

tequila

Margarita Cocktail
1 1/2 oz tequila
1/2 oz triple sec
1 oz lime juice
salt

Place salt in a saucer. Rub the rim of a cocktail glass with lime wedge and dip the glass into salt to coat rim thoroughly. Pour the ingredients into a cocktail shaker half filled with ice cubes.

Serve in: Margarita glass or cocktail glass

Melon Margarita
2 tsp coarse salt
2 oz tequila
2 oz Midori ® melon liqueur
1/2 oz lime juice

Place salt in a saucer. Rub the rim of a cocktail glass with lime wedge and dip the glass into salt to coat rim thoroughly. Shake the tequila, Midori and lime juice with ice cubes in a cocktail shaker. Strain into the rimmed glass, and serve.

Serve in: Margarita glass or cocktail glass

Olive Margarita
1 1/2 oz gold tequila
1 1/2 oz rosso vermouth
1 dash Blue Curacao® liqueur
1 green olive

Pour equal parts tequila and sweet vermouth into a cocktail shaker with ice. Add the curacao, and shake well. Strain into a cocktail glass and drop in an olive.

Serve in: Margarita glass or cocktail glass

Orange Margarita
3/4 oz triple sec
1 oz Jose Cuervo® gold tequila
1 oz freshly squeezed lime juice
1/2 oz fresh orange juice

Shake all ingredients together in a cocktail shaker half filled with ice, and strain into cocktail glass. Garnish with fresh orange and lime slices.

Serve in: Margarita glass or cocktail glass

tequila

tequila

Something for the Weekend

1 1/2 oz tequila
1/2 oz dark creme de cacao
1 oz heavy cream
1/2 tsp Chambord® raspberry liqueur
fresh raspberries for garnish
sprig of mint

Pour tequila, dark creme de cacao, heavy cream and Chambord into a cocktail shaker half filled with ice cubes. Shake, strain into a cocktail glass and garnish with fresh raspberries and sprig of mint.

Serve in: Cocktail glass

Tequila Shot

1 oz gold tequila
1 pinch salt
1 lime wedge

Hold the lime between your finger and thumb, and place a pinch of salt at the base of the thumb on the same hand. Quickly lick the salt, down the tequila, and suck the lime.

Serve in: Shot glass

Angels Above

1 1/2 oz dark rum
1 oz Amaretto® almond liqueur
1 1/2 oz whipping cream
1/2 tsp sifted cocoa powder

Place all of the ingredients into a cocktail shaker with a handful of ice cubes and shake well. Strain into a cocktail glass.

Serve in: Cocktail glass

Ataboy

2 oz white rum
2 oz fresh cream
1/2 oz Grand Marnier®
1/2 oz Galliano®
1 dash grenadine syrup
maraschino cherry (optional) for garnish

Pour the white rum, cream, Grand Marnier, Galliano and grenadine into a cocktail shaker half filled with ice. Shake well. Strain into a cocktail glass and garnish with a maraschino cherry, and serve.

Serve in: Cocktail glass

Bahama Mama

1/4 oz coffee liqueur
1/2 oz dark rum
1/2 oz coconut liqueur
juice of 1/2 lemon
4 oz pineapple juice
maraschino cherry (optional) for garnish
strawberry (optional) for garnish

Mix all of the ingredients together in a mixing glass and pour over cracked ice in a collins glass. Decorate with a strawberry or cherry and serve.

Serve in: Collins Glass

Bahia Baby

3/4 oz dark rum
1/2 oz spiced rum
2 1/2 oz pineapple juice
1 oz coconut cream
pineapple (optional) for garnish

Half fill a cocktail shaker with ice and pour in all of the ingredients. Shake well and strain into a collins glass filled with crushed ice. Garnish with a pineapple wedge.

Serve in: Collins glass

rum

Bali High

1/2 oz coconut rum
1 oz lime juice
2 oz passion-fruit juice
2 oz fizzy orange
1/2 oz pineapple syrup

Half fill a cocktail shaker with ice and pour in all of the ingredients except the fizzy orange. Shake well and strain into an ice filled collins glass. Top-up with fizzy orange.

Serve in: Collins glass

Banana Daiquiri

1 1/2 oz light rum
1 tbsp triple sec
1 banana
1 1/2 oz lime juice
1 tsp sugar
maraschino cherry (optional) for garnish

Combine all ingredients in a blender with half a cup of crushed ice and blend until smooth. Pour into a champagne flute, and top with the cherry.

Serve in: Champagne flute

Beach Comber

1 1/4 oz spiced rum
4 oz pineapple juice
3 oz cranberry juice
pineapple (optional) for garnish

Pour the spiced rum, pineapple juice and cranberry juice into a cocktail shaker half filled with ice cubes. Shake well and strain into a collins glass filled with ice cubes, garnish with a pineapple wedge, and serve.

Serve in: Collins glass

Bee's Knees

1 oz white rum
1/4 oz dark rum
3/4 oz cream
2 tsp honey

Combine all of the ingredients over crushed ice in a shaker. Shake well, strain into a cocktail glass, and serve.

Serve in: Cocktail glass

Cabana Club

1 oz rum
1/2 oz coconut cream
1 oz pineapple juice
1 oz cranberry juice
1 dash grenadine syrup

Blend with crushed ice.

Serve in: Hurricane glass

Caribbean Breeze

1 oz Bacardi® rum
1/2 oz Malibu® coconut rum
2oz pineapple juice
2oz cranberry juice

In a mixing glass, stir the Barcardi, Malibu and juices. Pour the ingredients into a collins glass filled with ice.

Serve in: Collins glass

rum

Caribbean Delight

2 oz orange juice
1 oz rum
1 oz peach schnapps
1 dash grenadine syrup

Combine the ingredients in a shaker half filled with ice and shake well. Strain over ice into a highball glass.

Serve in: Highball glass

Caribbean Kiss

2 oz dark rum
1 oz Amaretto®
1 oz Kahlua®
2 oz cream
cinnamon
brown sugar

Rub the rim of a cocktail glass into the Kahlua, and dip into a saucer of brown sugar. Shake the spirits and cream with ice in a cocktail shaker then, strain into a chilled cocktail glass. Decorate by sprinkling with cinnamon.

Serve in: Cocktail glass

Caribbean Princess

1 1/2 oz watermelon schnapps
1/2 oz Malibu® coconut rum
1 1/2 oz triple sec
5 oz orange juice
3 oz lemonade
1/2 oz lemon juice

Place all of the ingredients in a mixing glass and stir gently. Pour into a collins glass with handful of ice.

Serve in: Collins glass

Cast Away

3 oz Captain Morgan® coconut rum
1 oz banana liqueur
2 oz orange juice
pineapple (optional) for garnish
maraschino cherry (optional) for garnish

Pour all the ingredients into a highball glass. Add crushed ice until full, and garnish and serve.

Serve in: Highball glass

Cuba Libra

1 - 2 oz dark rum
1 fresh lime or lemon
Coca-Cola®

Fill a glass with ice cubes then add
rum. Cut the lime in half and rub
the edge of lime on the rim of
glass. Cut a slice off one half of
the lime to use as garnish then
squeeze the remaining lime juice
into glass. Fill with Coca-Cola, stir
and garnish with the slice of lime.

Serve in: Collins glass

Elegant Lips

1 1/2 oz dark rum
1/2 oz creme de bananes
1/2 oz lemon juice

Combine all of the ingredients in a
cocktail shaker half filled with ice
cubes and shake well. Strain into a
cocktail glass.

Serve in: Cocktail glass

Friday's Child

3/4 oz white rum
3/4 oz mango syrup
1/4 mango
1/4 oz lime juice

Put the chopped mango in a blender with the rum and mango syrup and a cup of rum crushed ice. Blend until smooth then strain into a large glass, and fill with crushed ice. Squeeze in a lime wedge, and serve.

Serve in: Highball glass

Fruit Loop

1/2 oz banana liqueur
1/2 oz dark rum
1/2 oz Midori® melon liqueur
1/2 oz peach schnapps
1 dash creme de cassis
1 dash grenadine syrup
6 oz pineapple juice
pineapple (optional) for garnish

Pour the banana liqueur, dark rum, Midori melon liqueur, peach schnapps, creme de cassis and grenadine into a collins glass filled with ice cubes. Fill with pineapple juice, garnish with a slice of pineapple, and serve.

Serve in: Collins glass

Green Goddess

3/4 oz Midori® melon liqueur
1 oz rum
1/2 oz Rose's® lime juice
1/2 oz cream of coconut
1 1/2 oz pineapple juice

Combine all of the ingredients in a cocktail shaker half filled with ice. Shake well and then strain into a chilled cocktail glass.

Serve in: Cocktail glass

Happy Hawaiian

2 1/4 oz Malibu®
4 1/2 oz cherry cola
1 1/2 oz pineapple juice
1 1/2 oz lemonade
pineapple (optional) for garnish

Pour the ingredients into a glass with a handful of ice cubes then stir well. Garnish with a slice of pineapple.

Serve in: Collins glass

Honey Bunny
2 oz Jamaican dark rum
1/4 oz honey
1/2 oz lemon juice

Pour the rum, honey and lemon juice into a cocktail shaker half filled with ice cubes. Shake well, strain into a cocktail glass, and serve.

Serve in: Cocktail glass

Just So
1/2 oz Malibu® coconut rum
1 oz white creme de cacao
1 oz white creme de menthe

Combine all ingredients with ice, shake, and strain into old-fashioned glass.

Serve in: Old-Fashioned glass

Karma Lama
2 oz dark rum
1 oz simple syrup (see pp21)
1 oz lime juice

Pour ingredients into an old-fashioned glass 3/4 filled with crushed ice.

Serve in: Old-Fashioned glass

Little White Lie

1 1/2 oz white rum
1 oz lychee wine
1/2 oz lime juice
1/2 oz passion-fruit juice

Mix together in a cocktail shaker half filled with ice, shake well and strain into a glass.

Serve in: Cocktail glass

Mai Tai

3oz white rum
3oz dark rum
1 1/2 oz Orange Curacao® liqueur
1 1/2 oz Orgeat syrup
1 oz fresh lime juice

Combine all the ingredients (except the dark rum) together in a cocktail shaker half filled with ice. Shake well and strain into a tall glass. Float the dark rum onto the top.

Orgeat syrup is a sweet syrup made from almonds, sugar and rose water/ orange-flower water. It has a pronounced almond taste. Orgeat syrup can be hard to find, but if you can't find it, almond syrup is a good substitute.

Serve in: Collins glass

Mojito

1/2 oz light rum
3 fresh mint sprigs
2 tsp sugar
3 tbsp fresh lime juice
soda water

Crush half of the mint with a fork on the inside of the glass. Add the sugar and lime juice and stir thoroughly. Add ice cubes then add the rum and mix. Fill the glass with soda water then add a lime slice and the remaining mint.

Serve in: Collins glass

Naughty Naughty

1 1/2 oz light rum
1 oz orange juice
1/2 oz lemon juice
ginger ale

Combine all the ingredients (except ginger ale) with ice in a cocktail shaker and shake well. Strain into a glass over ice cubes and fill with ginger ale.

Serve in: Collins glass

rum

Pina Colada

3 oz Malibu®
3 oz pineapple juice
3 tbsp coconut cream
pineapple (optional) for garnish
soda water

Combine ingredients in a mixing glass with crushed ice. Mix well and strain into a highball glass. Garnish with a slice of fresh pineapple, and serve. If you find the consistency too rich you can add soda water to taste.

Serve in: Hurricane glass

Say Something Tropical

1 oz Malibu® coconut rum
1 oz Midori® melon liqueur
1 1/2 oz pineapple juice
1/2 oz whipped cream

Pour ingredients over ice in a cocktail shaker. Shake until blended, pour into an old-fashioned glass, and serve.

Serve in: Old Fashioned glass

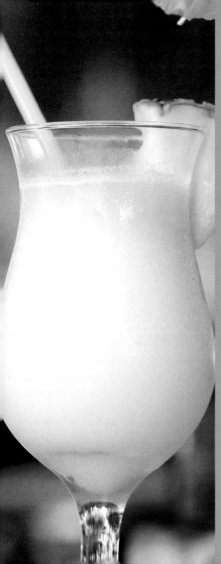

Tahitian Beauty

1 oz Bacardi® Limon rum
1 oz Amaretto® almond liqueur
4 oz cranberry juice
lemonade

Fill a glass with ice and then add the Barcardi Limon followed by the Amaretto, the cranberry juice and lemonade in order.

Serve in: Highball glass

Tropical Dream

1 oz Malibu® coconut rum
1 oz banana schnapps
1 oz Stoli® Vanil vodka
2 oz orange juice
2 oz pineapple juice
1 splash grenadine syrup

Half fill a cocktail shaker with ice and pour in all of the ingredients except the grenadine. Shake well and strain into a hurricane glass filled with ice. Float grenadine on top, and serve with a cherry garnish.

Serve in: Hurricane glass

rum

Black Russian

3 oz vodka

3 oz Kahlua® coffee liqueur

Coca-Cola®

1 lime wedge

Pour the vodka and the Kahlua into a tall glass over ice. Top with coke and serve with the wedge of lime.

Serve in: Highball glass

Bloody Mary

3 oz vodka

6 oz tomato juice

2 oz lemon juice

1 tsp Worcestershire® sauce

4 - 6 drops Tabasco® sauce

1 dash celery salt

1 lime wedge

celery for garnish plus salt and pepper

Shake all ingredients (except lime wedge) with ice in a cocktail shaker and shake well. Strain into a glass over ice cubes. Add salt and pepper to taste and the wedge of lime and celery for garnish.

Serve in: Highball glass

Campari Martini
3 oz vodka
1 oz Campari® bitters

Pour into a cocktail shaker half filled with ice, shake well, and strain into a chilled cocktail glass. Garnish with a twist of lime.

Serve in: Cocktail glass

Chocolate Martini
1 1/2 oz Stoli® Vanil vodka
1 oz Godiva® chocolate liqueur
1 maraschino cherry

Mix the vodka and chocolate liqueur in shaker filled with ice. Strain into either a wine glass or martini glass and garnish with a cherry.

Serve in: Wine glass

Dirty Dog
3 oz vodka
1 oz cherry brandy
1/2 oz Campari® bitters

Pour all of the ingredients into a cocktail shaker half filled with ice. Shake well. Strain into a chilled cocktail glass, garnish with a lemon twist, and serve.

Harvey Wallbanger
1 oz vodka
1/2 oz Galliano® herbal liqueur
4 oz orange juice

Pour the vodka and orange juice
into a tall glass over ice cubes and
stir. Float the Galliano on top.

Serve in: Collins glass

Kamikaze
1 oz vodka
1 oz triple sec
1 oz lime juice

Shake all of the ingredients with ice
in a cocktail shaker and then strain
into an old-fashioned glass over ice
cubes.

Serve in: Old-Fashioned glass

Screwdriver

2 oz vodka
5 oz orange juice

Put 3 ice cubes into a tall glass then pour in the vodka. Top up the glass with orange juice, stir, and serve.

Serve in: Highball glass

Sex on the Beach

1 1/2 oz vodka
3/4 oz peach schnapps
1/2 oz creme de cassis
2 oz orange juice
2 oz cranberry juice
orange slice for garnish
maraschino cherry for garnish

Pour all the ingredients into a shaker with ice cubes and shake well. Strain into tall glass and garnish with the orange slice and maraschino cherry.

Serve in: Highball glass

Vodka Martini
1 1/2 oz vodka
3/4 oz dry vermouth

Shake vodka and vermouth together with ice cubes in a shaker and shake well. Strain into a cocktail glass, garnish with an olive and serve.

Serve in: Cocktail glass

Voodoo Smile
1/2 oz vodka
1/2 oz Chambord® raspberry liqueur
orange juice & cranberry juice

Add vodka and Chambord to a shaker. Add orange juice and cranberry juice until desired taste. Shake and serve with ice in a cocktail glass.

Serve in: Cocktail glass

Woo Woo
1 1/2 oz peach schnapps
1 1/2 oz vodka
3 1/2 oz cranberry juice

Pour all ingredients into a highball glass over ice cubes, stir, and serve.

Serve in: Highball glass

Deadly Assassin.

2 oz whiskey
2 - 3 dashes sambuca
1 oz dry vermouth
1 oz soda water
1 oz pineapple juice

Pour the vermouth, whiskey and pineapple juice together in a cocktail shaker half filled with ice and shake well. Pour into a collins glass, and top it off with soda water and finally the sambuca on top.

Serve in: Collins Glass

Jumping Jack

4 oz Jack Daniel's® Tennessee whiskey
8 oz Coca-Cola®
2 tsp grenadine syrup
1 maraschino cherry

Pour the Jack Daniel's into a tall glass filled with ice cubes. Pour Coca-cola into the glass, and add the grenadine. Stir lightly and garnish with a cherry.

Serve in: Highball glass

Loch Ness Monster

3/4 oz Scotch whiskey
1/4 oz apricot brandy
1 dash Orange Curacao® liqueur
2 oz grapefruit juice
1/4 oz lime juice

Pour all of the ingredients into a cocktail shaker half filled with ice. Shake well and strain into a collins glass filled with crushed ice. Garnish with a lime wedge.

Serve in: Collins glass

Maggie May Not

1 oz Kahlua® coffee liqueur
1 oz whiskey
4 oz milk

Pour the Kahlua into an old-fashioned glass with ice cubes. Add the milk and whiskey and stir well.

Serve in: Old-fashioned glass

Manhattan

1 1/4 oz rye whiskey
1/2 oz sweet vermouth
2 - 3 dashes Angostura bitters
maraschino cherry for garnish

Pour the ingredients into a mixing glass with ice cubes. Stir well and strain into a chilled cocktail glass. Garnish with the cherry.

Serve in: Cocktail glass

Mint Julep

4 oz bourbon
4 - 6 mint leaves
2 sugar cubes
mint sprig for garnish

Place the ingredients into a cocktail shaker. Crush the sugar cubes, mint and bourbon well to dissolve the sugar and to release the oil and aroma of the mint. Add ice cubes to the shaker and shake well. Strain into a julep cup or collins glass with ice cubes. Garnish with the mint sprig.

Serve in: Collins glass

Old-fashioned

1 sugar cube
2 - 3 dashes Angostura bitters
2 orange slices
2 oz bourbon
1/2 oz soda water
maraschino cherry for garnish

Place the sugar cube at the bottom of an old-fashioned glass and add the bitters. Add one orange slice and crush these together. Fill the glass with ice cubes then add the bourbon and the soda water. Stir well and garnish with a second orange slice and a maraschino cherry.

Serve in: Old-Fashioned glass

Rusty Nail

1 1/2 oz Scotch whiskey
3/4 oz Drambuie
lemon twist for garnish

Pour the ingredients into an old-fashioned glass with ice cubes. Stir well and garnish with the lemon twist.

Serve in: Old-Fashioned glass

Whiskey Breath

4 oz Scotch whiskey
12 oz dry ginger
3 - 4 drops Angostura® bitters
1 piece ginger

Crush a small piece of fresh ginger in a tall glass to release the flavour. Fill the glass with ice then add the whiskey and ginger ale. Drop in a strip of lemon peel and stir gently.

Serve in: Collins glass

Whiskey Sour

2 oz whiskey
2 oz lemon juice
2 oz simple syrup (see below)
5 ice cubes
1 lemon rind

Pour the ingredients into a cocktail shaker half filled with ice and shake well. Strain into a tall glass with the ice cubes. To make the simple syrup you will need 2 parts sugar and 1 part water. Bring the water to a boil and dissolve the sugar in the water. Once the sugar is dissolved completely, remove the pan from the heat and allow to cool.

Serve in: Collins glass

Champagne Based

Alice in Wonderland, pp 14
Baby Love, pp 14
Bellini, pp 17
Black Velvet, pp 17
Blitz, pp 17
Blue Tahoe, pp 18
Bolli Stoli, pp 18
Champagne Cocktail, pp 19
Champagne Fizz, pp 19
Champagne Punch, pp 20
Classic Champagne Cocktail, pp 20
Fizzy Fuzzy Navel, pp 20
Grand Mimosa, pp 21
Happy Hangover, pp 21
Kir Royale, pp 23
Mimosa, pp 23
Pink Drink, pp 24
Raspberry Shine, pp 24
Rose of the Ritz, pp 25
Strawberry Kir Royale, pp 25
Strawberry Champagne, pp 26
Tropical Champagne Kiss, pp 26

Gin Based

American Star, pp 28
Angel's Delight, pp 28
Aperitivo, pp 29
Blue Moon Martini, pp 29
Dirty Martini, pp 29
Dry Martini, pp 30
Gimlet, pp 30
Gin Fizz, pp 33
Long Island Iced Tea, pp 33
Negroni Cocktail, pp 34
Perfect 10, pp 34

Pimm's Cup, pp 35
Pineapple Plaza, pp 35
Pink Lady, pp 37
Pixie Stick, pp 37
Raspberry Release, pp 37
Red Lion, pp 38
Silver King, pp 38
Singapore Sling, pp 39
Sloe Comfortable Screw, pp 39
Sloe Comfortable Screw, Again, pp 40
Sloe Gin Fizz, pp 40
Sloeberry Cocktail, pp 41
Slow Screw, pp 41
Smile Cocktail, pp 41
Spicy Martini, pp 42
Snake In The Grass, pp 42
Strawberry Martini, pp 44
Super Supreme, pp 44
Raspberry Martini, pp 45
Tailspin Charlie, pp 47
Tanqueray and Tonic, pp 47
Tom Collins, pp 48
Try As I Might, pp 48
Tuxedo Junction, pp 49
Venom, pp 49
Waikiki Woo, pp 50
Wedding Bells, pp 50
White Gin Smoothie, pp 50
Wimbledon Cup, pp 51
Wonder Why?, pp 51

Tequila Based

Acapulco Vision, pp 52
Aztec Gold, pp 52
Banana Margarita, pp 54
Black Monday, pp 54
Charlie's Angel, pp 55
Cranberry Margarita, pp 55
Frozen Margarita, pp 56
Frozen Strawberry Margarita, pp 56
Fuzzy Pierced Navel, pp 58
Gold Margarita, pp 58
High Velocity, pp 59
Highland Margarita, pp 59
Italiano Margarita, pp 60
Love Child, pp 60
Margarita Cocktail, pp 62
Melon Margarita, pp 62
Olive Margarita, pp 63
Orange Margarita, pp 63
Something for the Weekend, pp 65
Tequila Shot, pp 65

Rum Based

Angels Above, pp 66
Ataboy, pp 66
Bahama Mama, pp 67
Bahia Baby, pp 67
Bali High, pp 68
Banana Daiquiri, pp 68

index

Rum Based/Cont.

Beach Comber, pp 70
Bee's Knees, pp 70
Cabana Club, pp 71
Caribbean Breeze, pp 71
Caribbean Delight, pp 72
Caribbean Kiss, pp 72
Caribbean Princess, pp 74
Cast Away, pp 74
Cuba Libra, pp 75
Elegant Lips, pp 75
Friday's Child, pp 76
Fruit Loop, pp 76
Green Goddess, pp 77
Happy Hawaiian, pp 77
Honey Bunny, pp 78
Just So, pp 78
Karma Lama, pp 78
Little White Lie, pp 79
Mai Tai, pp 79
Mojito, pp 81
Naughty Naughty, pp 81
Pina Colada, pp 82
Say Something Tropical, pp 82
Tahitian Beauty, pp 83
Tropical Dream, pp 83

Vodka Based

Campari Martini, pp 86
Chocolate Martini, pp 86
Dirty Dog, pp 86
Harvey Wallbanger, pp 87
Kamikaze, pp 87
Screwdriver, pp 88
Sex on the Beach, pp 88
Vodka Martini, pp 89
Voodoo Smile, pp 89
Woo Woo, pp 89

Whiskey based

Deadly Assassin, pp 90
Jumping Jack, pp 90
Loch Ness Monster, pp 91
Maggie May Not, pp 91
Manhattan, pp 92
Mint Julip, pp 92
Old-fashioned, pp 93
Rusty Nail, pp 93
Whiskey Breath, pp 94
Whiskey Sour, pp 94

Publishers Disclaimer

This edition published in 2008 by Bizzybee Publishing Ltd.
© bizzybee publishing 2008 Printed in China